MG 8.7 lpt.

THE CITY

Text: Rosa Costa-Pau
Illustrations: Estudio Marcel Socías

La Salvaguardia de las Ciudades © Copyright
Parramón Ediciones, S. A. Published by
Parramón Ediciones, S. A., Barcelona, Spain.

1 3 5 7 9 8 6 4 2

Ciudad. English
   The city
      p. cm.—(The Junior library of ecology)
   Translation of: La Ciudad.
   Includes index.
   Summary: Introduces the environmental
problems which affect life in cities.
   ISBN   0-7910-2101-7
   1. Urban ecology—Juvenile literature. 2.
Cities and towns—Juvenile literature. [1.
Urban ecology. 2. Cities and towns. 3. Ecology.]
I. Chelsea House Publishers. II. Title. III.
Series.
HT241.C5813 1994   93-17918
307.76—dc20   CIP
                                          AC

Contents

The Junior Library of Ecology

THE CITY

3390

CHELSEA HOUSE PUBLISHERS

New York • Philadelphia

The Origin of Towns and Cities

Hunters and Farmers

A long time ago when large and ferocious animals inhabited the earth, hunting was a dangerous activity only undertaken by the strongest of the young people. When we examine the life of the hunter, it is easy to see how survival depended upon the resources that occurred spontaneously in nature: minerals, plants, and animals. When humans discovered agriculture, however, animals who lived on the land that people had begun to cultivate were forced to look for food and water elsewhere.

Primitive humans observed the animals' habits and instead of killing them, domesticated them, which brought great benefits. Humans became livestock farmers.

The First Villages

The first villages were established when groups of people ceased to live a nomadic life, and were faced with the need to remain in the same place for a long time while waiting for the planted seeds to produce a crop.

When agriculture and livestock provided the means of survival, people began to have more time to spend on social activities and pastimes such as music, painting, and art.

Life became richer and more varied, but also more complex. The need for defense and mutual aid motivated people to build the first villages. These early villages were located on top of small hills, places which were difficult to reach and easy to defend. It was only when humanity's work became more complex that large cities began to develop.

▲
The human race has lived a large part of its history in nomadic tribes and small villages.

The first walled cities appeared in the 11th century. At that time London, the largest English city, had sixteen thousand inhabitants. ▶

When it became necessary to find places to store crops and pen livestock, the first settlements appeared. ▼

The first villages were located close to rivers, which supplied water, and to forests, which supplied building materials and firewood. ▼

The increase in the population that occurred around the 12th century and the concentration of people in the early cities brought about a considerable reduction in the forests.

In the 17th century, forests were greatly exploited. Wood was a source of energy and building material during the early industrial revolution.

In the 19th century, there were already many cities with more than one hundred thousand inhabitants.

▲

The movement of crops and other products from the countryside to the cities gave rise to the first systems of transport and communication.

The Development of Large Cities

The Population

The human population, like animal and plant life, is not equally distributed throughout the world. There are areas where population density is high and other extensive areas where very few people or none at all live. In general, population is less dense in rural areas than in towns and cities.

Population Growth

Natural population growth is the difference between the number of people born and those who die over a given period. If the number of births is greater than the number of deaths, the population increases.

But this has not always occurred. For the population to increase, the mortality rate must decrease. This is what has happened in recent years thanks to improved diet, health care, sanitation, personal hygiene, and environmental protection.

The population has been able to increase because the necessary natural resources have been available. The survival of the first villages was made possible by collaboration between groups of peoples who searched for food together and defended themselves against natural difficulties.

In the past, humans lived like the other nomadic animals. People lived off the resources around them and then moved on to another territory, where they could start again. ▼

Throughout history, the characteristics of houses have varied according to human needs. ▼

The agricultural villages grew much more rapidly than the hunting and gathering villages. ►

As farmers began to produce more food, they needed places to store it and a marketplace to exchange it for other products—hence the growth of villages.

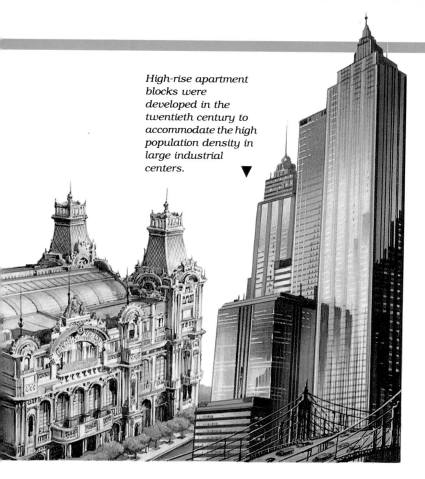

High-rise apartment blocks were developed in the twentieth century to accommodate the high population density in large industrial centers. ▼

Human Population and Resource Use

By studying the increase in the human population and humanity's increased capacity to exploit and control natural resources, we can obtain a clearer idea of how this increase came about and what impact this had on the environment.

One of the characteristics of the human race is its capacity to develop means of transport. This has allowed a great part of humanity to free itself from the nomadic lifestyle that was the norm in the past.

In all ecosystems, energy and matter are transported and circulate from one place to another. The life forms that take an active part in organizing this transport have always obtained certain advantages.

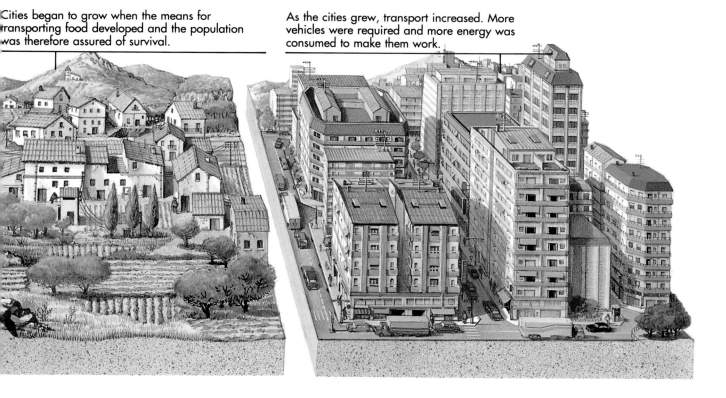

Cities began to grow when the means for transporting food developed and the population was therefore assured of survival.

As the cities grew, transport increased. More vehicles were required and more energy was consumed to make them work.

The City, an Ecosystem

An Unusual Ecosystem

The city can be considered to be a special kind of ecosystem. In the city, like in any other ecosystem, both plant and animal organisms are found, but here humans are the dominant species.

Organisms relate to each other and the surrounding environment through an exchange of matter and energy. In the city, however, these exchanges have special characteristics because of the physical framework—the urban structure—in which they occur, and because of the enormous amount of energy circulating within this ecosystem.

Birds such as the swift and the swallow, insects, and even some mammals such as the bat live in the sky over the city.

Similarities exist between cities that are very distant from each other. Houses are heated and cooled with the same sort of air-conditioning and heating systems that can be installed in any part of the world.

Rubbish dumps are dangerous places to live, but they are also a rich source of nutrients, so that some plants, beetles, and rats thrive there.

In abandoned city lots, animals and wild plants such as thistle and nettle are able to survive and propagate.

Highway and road systems facilitate the movement of materials, but also cause congestion and pollution.

As in a lake or forest, the physical and biological elements that make up a city's ecosystem are related. They transform the physical environment and adapt themselves to it at the same time.

In the city human beings consume and produce, but above all they produce waste.

◀ There are many plants and animals in cities that have been brought in for decorative purposes: trees, cats and dogs, a great variety of flowering plants, and some kinds of birds.

Physical Elements

The environmental and physical surroundings of cities have certain characteristics that are created by the urban structure. This urban structure is made up of buildings, streets, gas and water pipes, electric lines, transportation systems, and so on.

The elements that determine the climate of this ecosystem, such as temperature, humidity, wind, and atmospheric pressure, are to a great extent altered by the urban structure, so that their behavior differs from those of nearby non-urban ecosystems. For example, buildings alter the effects of solar radiation and air circulation, and asphalt streets heat up more quickly than the forest floor or the surface of the sea or lakes. The air in the city is also heated by the gases emitted by motor vehicles, domestic heating systems, and industry.

The urban structure of the city has always been planned in close relationship with climatic conditions, type of land or substratum, and the available construction materials.

Biological Elements

The biological element of this ecosystem includes all the life forms that inhabit a large city: plants, animals, and human beings. There is very little variety in the flora and fauna that live in cities owing to the lack of habitable space and to the fact that it is a polluted, intensively exploited environment.

In spite of this, some species are adapted to take advantage of conditions within cities. Ants, rats, roaches, and some birds are all organisms commonly found in this ecosystem. The flora and fauna that survive in a city are favored by humans, and they are mostly concentrated in parks and gardens.

Water

Essential for Life

Water is important because it is an excellent solvent for a great number of substances. Water transports nutrients throughout the body and is used to expel potentially harmful waste products. Water plays a part in all the chemical processes that take place in the body. Water is essential for life, for human beings, and for all living creatures.

Water, a Renewable Resource

There are currently more than six billion people living on the Earth. The exodus from rural areas to the cities means that most people live in large urban centers. The urban centers are zones with a very high population density.

This high density causes enormous problems because of the large quantity of resources required to maintain the population. These include non-renewable resources such as petroleum, and renewable resources such as water.

Water remains more or less constant in nature. It is a renewable resource because it can be constantly recycled. Because of the enormous consumption of water in large cities, human beings have invented mechanisms that interrupt and modify the natural cycle of water. People take water from a river or a reservoir, purify it, distribute it, use it, and dirty it. Sometimes this water is purified and returned to the sea but more often it reenters the natural cycle dirty and contaminated.

Water is a renewable resource, but it is subject to extreme chemical and biological transformations that threaten its usefulness and its role in natural processes.

Humans, Users of Water

The quantity of water that a city needs is calculated by taking into account the quantity of water needed by its inhabitants and industries.

City inhabitants consume water in the following proportions: 32% for food preparation, cleaning clothes, and washing dishes; 16% for toilets; 32% for personal hygiene; and the remaining 20% for watering gardens.

Increasing Use of Water

Water use in a city is determined by the number of inhabitants. In the last thirty years, water consumption in large cities has doubled. Today, a city of two million inhabitants needs close to one million cubic meters of water per day.

The water supply of a large city generally comes from reservoirs built on nearby rivers. Water comes from the reservoir as needed, and is distributed to homes and industries by means of aqueducts and pipes.

Pure water from lakes, reservoirs, or rivers is used by city inhabitants, contaminated, and purified before being discharged into the sea. ▼

Purified water is discharged into the sea.

Waste Water in the City

Water that has been used is channelled through a subterranean system and runs into the sea together with rainwater. After being used in a city, water has very different characteristics than in its natural state.

Waste water contains various kinds of substances. Some of these are products of organic activity, that is to say, they are produced by people themselves, while others are chemical substances that come from detergents and industrial processes.

Treatment of City Water

Water first goes through a purification process, then it travels through a city, and is finally returned, once again contaminated, to the river or the sea.

Water passing through its natural cycle can be purified, but the natural rhythm of this process is slower than the rate at which it is contaminated in cities. This is why water should be treated before it is returned to nature.

Waste water from factories and industries is purified before being returned to rivers. ▼

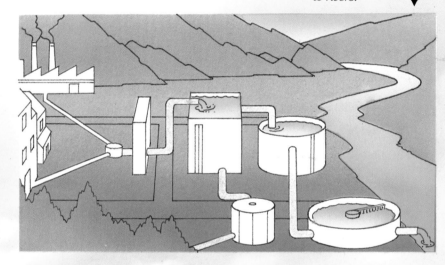

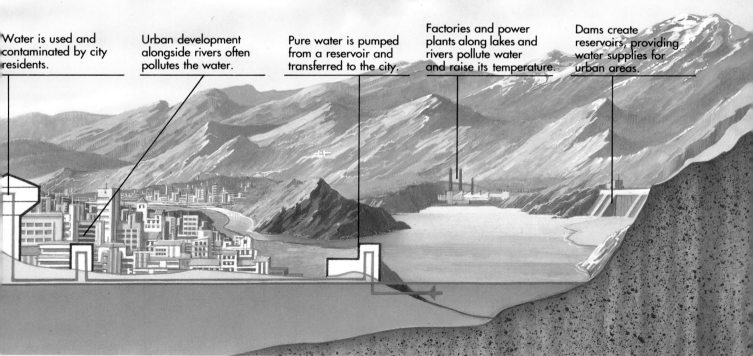

Water is used and contaminated by city residents.

Urban development alongside rivers often pollutes the water.

Pure water is pumped from a reservoir and transferred to the city.

Factories and power plants along lakes and rivers pollute water and raise its temperature.

Dams create reservoirs, providing water supplies for urban areas.

Air

Air in the City

Air is the gaseous mass that constitutes the Earth's atmosphere. It is this layer of air that protects all forms of life on Earth. Air is also an enormous oxygen reserve, thanks to which, we are able to live and breathe.

The composition of the atmosphere varies depending on the atmospheric layer or altitude. The air that constitutes the atmosphere of a large city also often has varying characteristics and components.

Air Pollution

Air is polluted when it contains foreign substances, or when the variation in its components produces a negative effect on people, animals, plants, and everything else.

The foreign substances and the alteration in the components of the air are usually caused by the activities carried out in the city itself. Smoke, dust, sulfur oxides, carbon monoxide and carbon dioxide, and heat and humidity are just some of the things that pollute city air. Each one of these elements has a greater or lesser effect, depending on the concentration present in the atmosphere.

City Smog

Domestic heating is responsible for much of the pollution in cities. The pollution level depends on the type of fuel being burned to heat houses and buildings.

If coal or oil is used, soot, ashes, carbon monoxide, nitrogen oxides, and sulfur dioxide are produced. The greatest danger from sulfur dioxide occurs when the humidity level is high. Moisture interacts with the sulfur dioxide to produce sulfuric acid.

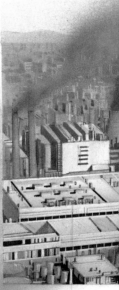

Sulfuric and other acids produced by combustion enter the atmosphere easily by combining with water droplets. When the acid content surpasses normal limits, it represents a threat to human health. ▶

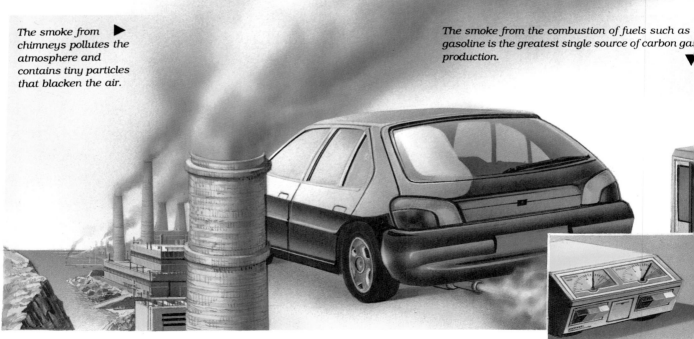

The smoke from ▶ chimneys pollutes the atmosphere and contains tiny particles that blacken the air.

The smoke from the combustion of fuels such as gasoline is the greatest single source of carbon ga. production. ▼

Effects on Human Health

The consequences of atmospheric pollution on human beings are little known and difficult to measure. City inhabitants constitute a varied population who live under a variety of different conditions. Changes in health are almost always due to a combination of causes.

Airborne acids dissolve limestone. Buildings and statues made of limestone or marble suffer from "stone sickness" and deteriorate little by little.

Building and monument cleanup campaigns inflate city maintenance budgets.

Public transport systems such as city buses carry a large number of people in a single vehicle. This helps keep the pollution levels down. ▼

Plant life in city parks and gardens helps keep the air cleaner and less polluted. ▼

Noise

Sound

Sound, like light, is an essential means of communication between human beings. Electromagnetic waves—light rays, radio waves, X rays, and infrared rays—do not require matter to propagate themselves. Sound is a mechanical wave because it cannot be produced in a vacuum and requires a material medium such as air, water, or earth to be propagated.

If we place a piece of paper or plastic on the membrane of a radio speaker, we can see it vibrate. Sound is produced by the vibration of physical bodies.

Sound Intensity

When vibrations in the air have a frequency of less than thirty cycles per second, we cannot perceive sound. This type of sound wave is called infrasonic. Ultrasound has frequencies greater than twenty thousand vibrations per second and is also imperceptible to the human ear.

The unit used to measure sound is the decibel. The sound level produced by falling leaves is ten decibels; the noise level of a quiet house or office is about forty decibels; and that of a street with heavy traffic is eighty decibels. When the sound level exceeds 120 decibels—the noise made by a pneumatic hammer—it causes pain in humans.

Noise has become an important factor in the large urban centers of the industrial world and noise pollution is now considered to be harmful to health. ▼

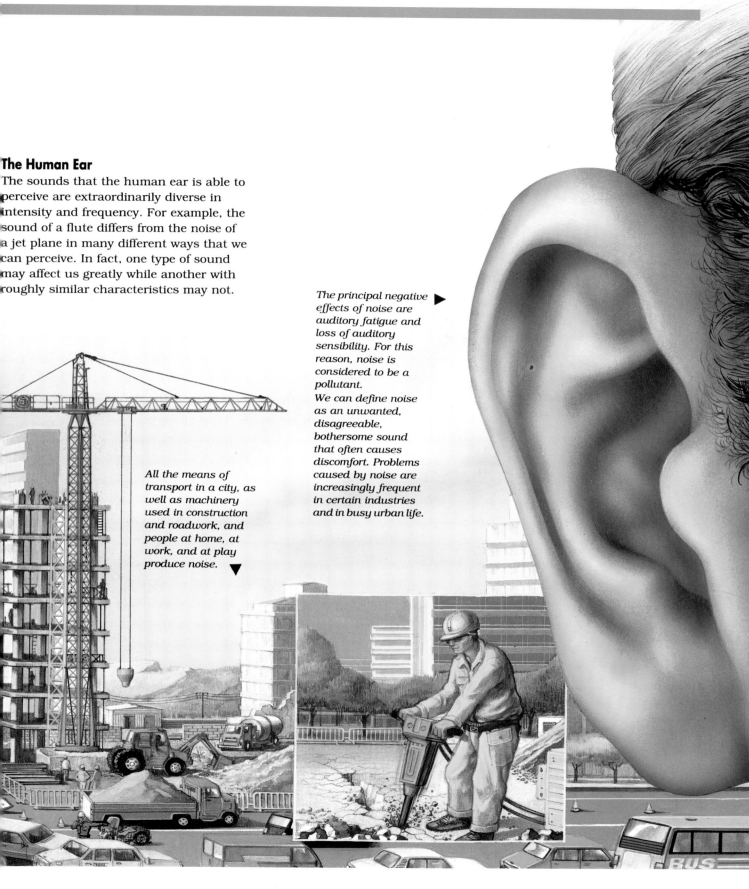

The Human Ear

The sounds that the human ear is able to perceive are extraordinarily diverse in intensity and frequency. For example, the sound of a flute differs from the noise of a jet plane in many different ways that we can perceive. In fact, one type of sound may affect us greatly while another with roughly similar characteristics may not.

The principal negative effects of noise are auditory fatigue and loss of auditory sensibility. For this reason, noise is considered to be a pollutant.
We can define noise as an unwanted, disagreeable, bothersome sound that often causes discomfort. Problems caused by noise are increasingly frequent in certain industries and in busy urban life. ▶

All the means of transport in a city, as well as machinery used in construction and roadwork, and people at home, at work, and at play produce noise. ▼

Climate

Weather in the Atmosphere

Atmospheric conditions include factors such as temperature, humidity, winds, clouds, and precipitation. Weather conditions can vary depending upon the location, the changing seasons, and the particular day. Some areas of the Earth are normally hotter than others; some have more rain and some even have continuous drought.

The average atmospheric conditions in a particular zone or region constitute the climate of the area. The climate can differ a great deal from one place to another.

One of the main reasons for this variation in climate is the spherical shape of the Earth. The intensity of solar energy striking a particular place varies according to the angle at which it strikes the surface. In far northern or southern regions, the angle of the sun's rays are more oblique and less solar energy is absorbed at the surface.

Modifications in the Urban Climate

The climates of cities are becoming increasingly different from rural climates because the structure of the city and the activities carried out in urban areas influence climatic factors.

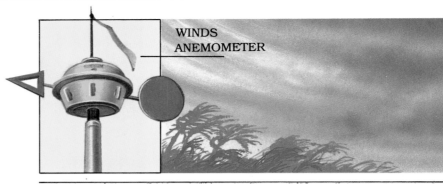

WINDS
ANEMOMETER

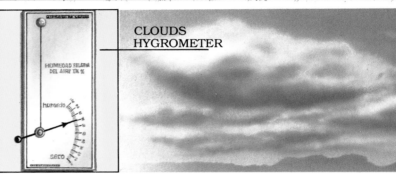

CLOUDS
HYGROMETER

PRECIPITATION
RAIN GAUGE

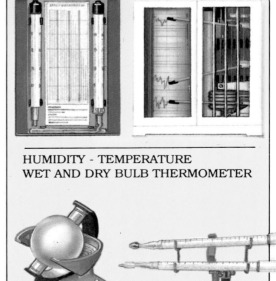

HUMIDITY - TEMPERATURE
WET AND DRY BULB THERMOMETER

Certain atmospheric phenomena such as humidity, wind, atmospheric pressure, and solar radiation affect the levels of air pollution. The information provided by meteorological stations can therefore be very useful.

The principal modifications in climate are:
- Reduction in wind velocity owing to the braking action of buildings on air movement.
- Less solar energy reaching the surface because of foreign substances (smoke, dust, ashes) in the atmosphere over the city.
- Higher temperatures due to heat accumulating in asphalt roads and stone buildings, as well as the heat produced by human activity.
- Lower relative humidity because trees and plant life have been replaced by asphalt and buildings.

Urban Climate and Pollution

Climatological conditions influence the distribution of atmospheric pollution. Wind disperses the pollution in a particular area and can transport it to another place, even over great distances. The formation of smog, therefore, is more likely under certain climatic conditions: strong sunlight and winds that are too light to adequately disperse the gaseous components of the smog. Thermal inversion is a meteorological phenomenon that contributes to urban pollution.

Warm air currents rise because they are less dense than the surrounding air. As such currents rise, they expand and cool.

When a rising air current reaches an altitude where it has the same temperature as the surrounding air mass, it stops rising.

The cold air is displaced towards a lower altitude.

The particular characteristics of air circulation in mountainous areas affect the pollution levels in nearby cities.

▼

The Living Beings of the City

Animal and Plant Life in the City

There are very few animal and plant species found in the city. The most important biological element in this ecosystem is people. The plants, animals, birds, and insects that live in the city pose no threat to the human inhabitants.

Creatures that have become urbanized, such as cats, dogs, canaries, and trees, are generally beneficial. There are, however, some forms of life, such as roaches, ants, and rats, that continue living and thriving in the city despite constant efforts by humans to exterminate them in various ways.

Refuges and Hideouts

Rats live beneath the city. They live in the underground sewers and come out to feed on the leftovers and waste products of the human inhabitants. Rats are adapted to live in a particular place in the city, so they are able to reproduce and survive easily.

Cities offer few possibilities for animal and plant life. Each species has to find its place, adapt, and then generally remain in that place for the rest of its life.

Some of the places that provide organisms with food and protection are abandoned lots, sidewalk trees, underground sewers, walls, roofs, and the sky above the city.

Humans continue to be the dominant creatures in the city. However, a number of animal and plant species survive and proliferate in urban environments. ▼

In parks and gardens, plants and animals reproduce under conditions very similar to those of a natural environment.

Parks and gardens are areas in a city reserved for rest and recreation. They are pleasant to look at and provide us with fresh clean air.

Trees and bushes thrive along the streets and in the squares of the city, making life more pleasant for the inhabitants.

Trees in parks shelter a great variety of life forms, such as birds, insects, fungus, and moss. All these life forms contribute to the growth of the trees.

Spiders use the webs they weave to hunt flying insects that nest in the bushes and in the holes of tree trunks.

Parks and Gardens

The areas of the city that most resemble nature are parks and gardens, where the greatest abundance of animal and plant life are found. Here we find trees such as willows, mimosa, and laurel; bushes such as rosebay, broom, and heather; and herbs and plants such as iris, geraniums, daisies, and grass.

City parks are often a small remaining part of what was once a forest. The parks sometimes conserve some of their original vegetation.

There are many well-adapted organisms in parks: fish such as the pond carp; birds such as the sparrow, starling, or pigeon; and a great variety of insects.

Food

Obtaining Food

In the past, the human race has withstood difficult conditions for a single reason: to obtain food for survival. This has been the most constant and important concern of all cultures. In ancient times, people lived by hunting, fishing, and gathering wild fruits.

Eventually, thanks to periods of abundant rainfall and the accumulation of knowledge acquired through experience, humans learned how to cultivate plants such as wheat and barley and domesticate animals such as dogs, goats, sheep, cows, and horses. This enabled human beings to control their food production.

Food Production

When more food was produced in some communities, not all of it was consumed by the inhabitants and there was often a surplus. It was no longer necessary for the entire population to take part in the production of food. Later, owing to further increases in urban population, farmers had to cultivate even larger areas of land.

Food Transport

Cities are often located far from agricultural areas. This makes it necessary to transport food products to commercial centers and markets. From there, the food products are distributed.

Farmers usually sell their products to intermediaries who then sell them in the city. There are shops, supermarkets, and shopping centers in the city where a large variety of products are available.

Food Conservation

Now, thanks to techniques like freezing, pasteurization, and the use of additives and preservatives, food is sold in the city in what is considered to be a fresh condition.

Today all kinds of food products can be marketed because of the development of preservation systems such as railroad tank cars and refrigerated trucks.

Raw materials such as wheat or milk generally go from the countryside to industrial centers where they are made into food products.

The transportation of ▶ food to the city raises the price of food. This price increase depends on factors such as the distance traveled, the quantity transported, and the ease of reaching the city.

THE REPLACEMENT OF FOREST BY CULTIVATED LAND

Controlled irrigation techniques are used to save water. Plants are often irrigated and fertilized simultaneously

The increase in population has produced an intensification of food cultivation and production. The cultivation of a single crop depletes the soil and promotes plant disease.

The processed food products are then transported to shops in the city and distributed among the population.

The massive use of air, land, and sea transport results in an increase in the price of food products as well as noise and pollution.

Energy Sources

Energy and Life

The sun is the principal energy source for all forms of life. However, only plants that contain chlorophyll are able to make direct use of organic materials through a process called photosynthesis.

Living beings that are not capable of photosynthesis obtain the energy they need to survive from the matter created by green plants. The solar energy converted by photosynthesizing plants is therefore used by other organisms in the food chain.

Interdependent relationships between different forms of life are established in order to obtain food and energy. Some creatures act as producers, and others as consumers.

Food Chains in the City

Humans are the dominant organism in the city. However, a large number of other small life forms also live there. As in any ecosystem, they establish relationships with each other and adapt to the urban environment.

Plants such as trees, moss, daisies, and dandelions are the producers in the city's food chain. The primary consumers of these foods include ants, plant lice, and the larvae of many insects. Secondary consumers feed off the primary consumers; therefore they indirectly depend on the producers. Lizards and sparrows are examples of secondary consumers. Domestic cats often hunt birds even though they receive food from their owners.

In the urban ecosystem, there is very little variety of life forms, and the amount of energy that moves through the food chains is slight.

External Energy

The quantity of material and energy that moves through the components of the urban ecosystem is considerably less than the amount of material and energy entering and leaving the city.

The city functions by consuming enormous quantities of energy obtained from outside the ecosystem. This is called external energy. The food that is consumed comes from the countryside. Electrical energy comes from large power stations. Fuel needed for industry and motor vehicles is extracted from subterranean deposits. Energy and materials are brought into the city by modern means of transport.

Surface Transport

Energy produced from coal, petroleum, and gas combustion in modern engines promotes the growth of land and sea transport. Products are taken from one place to another where they are consumed and the waste discarded. They are almost never returned to their place of origin. Therefore, in large cities, there is an enormous accumulation of residual waste products.

The flow of energy and materials within a city is similar to that of other ecosystems. Factories along rivers discharge waste materials into the water.

Industries also use water for cooling purposes, and the water they return to the river has a higher temperature.

Highways, bridges, and roads facilitate the movement of materials.

Energy is provided to power plants and transmitted to cities over long distances.

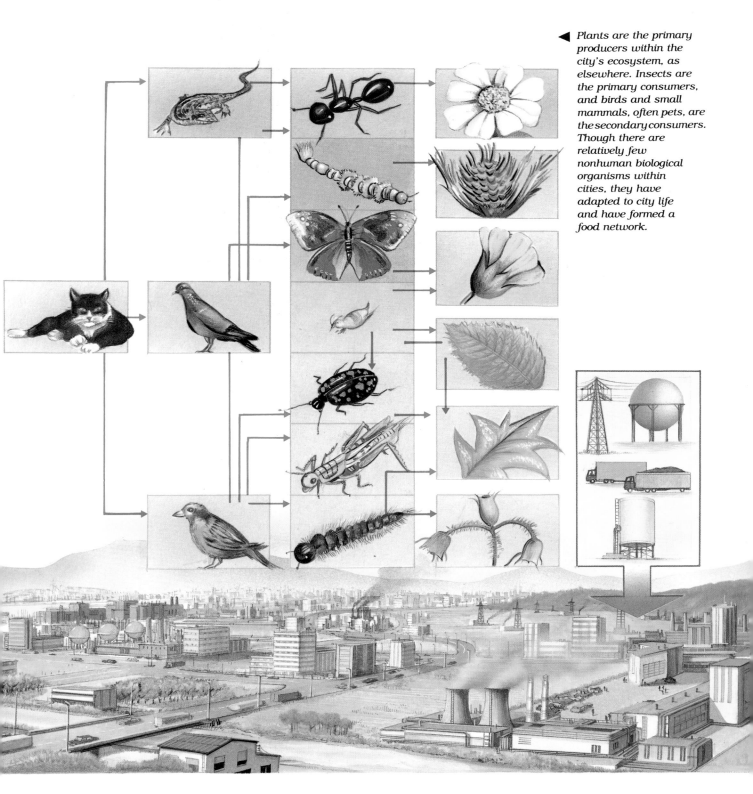

Plants are the primary producers within the city's ecosystem, as elsewhere. Insects are the primary consumers, and birds and small mammals, often pets, are the secondary consumers. Though there are relatively few nonhuman biological organisms within cities, they have adapted to city life and have formed a food network.

Waste Products

Incineration is a common process used to take advantage of waste products. Burned garbage gives off heat, which can be used to produce electricity.

Human Activity in the City

City life is similar to life inside an organism in that matter is continuously being transported in and out. The materials necessary for the growth and development of a living being are: air, water, food, and energy. Cities too need air, water, food, energy, and materials for producing or constructing buildings, houses, streets, and so on. These materials play a part in many urban processes. They are consumed by its inhabitants and they sometimes become consumer goods, such as tools, clothes, furniture, or machinery.

Solid Urban Waste

Another substance produced as a result of urban activity is called solid urban waste. Food wastes, packaging, discarded objects, plastic, wood, glass, tins, and cardboard boxes are some of the most common waste products. The accumulation of solid urban waste creates serious problems for cities.

In a typical city in the industrial world, an average family produces the following amount of waste in a year: 275 pounds of paper and cardboard; 185 pounds of glass; 120 pounds of plastic; and 750 pounds of metal.

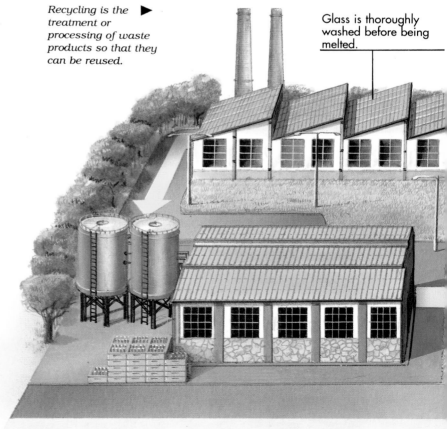

Recycling is the treatment or processing of waste products so that they can be reused.

Glass is thoroughly washed before being melted.

Plastics

Organic waste

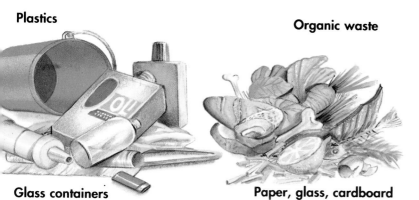

Glass containers

Paper, glass, cardboard

The Characteristics of Solid Urban Waste

Solid urban waste is removed from the city and is often transported to rubbish dumps, where it is eliminated or recycled. In the dumps of a large city, rubbish can be properly buried and covered with layers of earth. Sometimes it is burned or incinerated first.

▲

Compost, an excellent, high-quality organic fertilizer, is obtained by recycling vegetable and animal products and organic garbage.

New bottles, produced from the melted glass, are sold and reused.

The waste materials are first classified and separated.

Glass is one of the easiest inorganic materials to recycle.

How a City Functions

City Services

Shops, schools, hospitals, theaters, museums, post offices, telephones, and road systems are some of the most important urban services normally used by city inhabitants. Other key services, such as universities, central markets, train stations, airports, and government institutions, are also available.

Collective Services

In any city, there are many needs or problems common to the entire population that require a common solution. These problems are usually taken care of by the local authorities.

Collective services include posting signs on roads, garbage collection, water, electricity, gas, and urban transport. Low cost is characteristic of collective

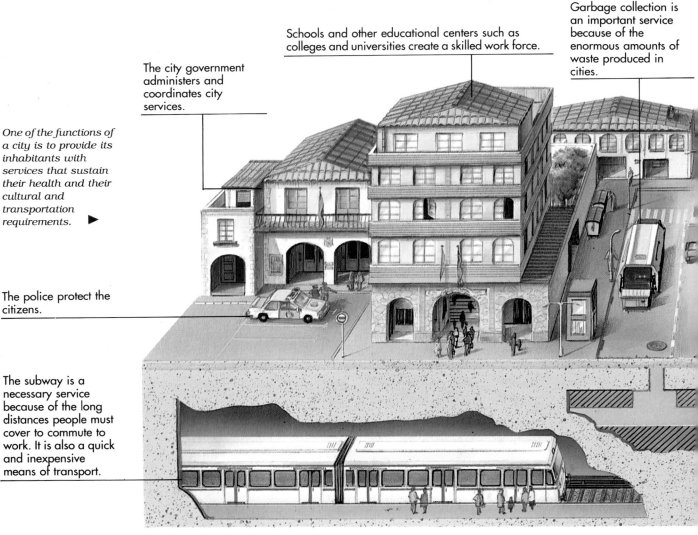

Schools and other educational centers such as colleges and universities create a skilled work force.

Garbage collection is an important service because of the enormous amounts of waste produced in cities.

The city government administers and coordinates city services.

One of the functions of a city is to provide its inhabitants with services that sustain their health and their cultural and transportation requirements. ▶

The police protect the citizens.

The subway is a necessary service because of the long distances people must cover to commute to work. It is also a quick and inexpensive means of transport.

Common Collective Services

The collective services of a city can also be grouped according to needs:
- Domestic needs include water, gas, and electricity.
- Urban needs include parking, transport, and traffic regulation.
- Social and cultural needs include education, sports activities, health services, and libraries.
- Protection needs include fire fighting services and the police.

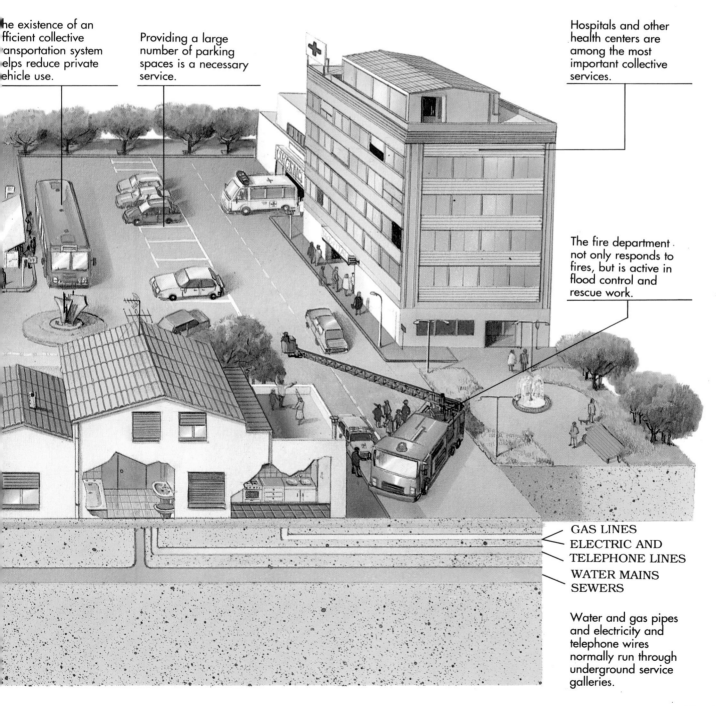

The existence of an efficient collective transportation system helps reduce private vehicle use.

Providing a large number of parking spaces is a necessary service.

Hospitals and other health centers are among the most important collective services.

The fire department not only responds to fires, but is active in flood control and rescue work.

GAS LINES
ELECTRIC AND TELEPHONE LINES
WATER MAINS
SEWERS

Water and gas pipes and electricity and telephone wires normally run through underground service galleries.

Activities

Cities receive their water through a network of subterranean pipes that drain water from distant reservoirs. It is important that the source of water be located at a higher elevation than the city, so that gravity can be used to make the water flow into the highest buildings. You can conduct an experiment to study how gravity can create water pressure with the following simple materials.

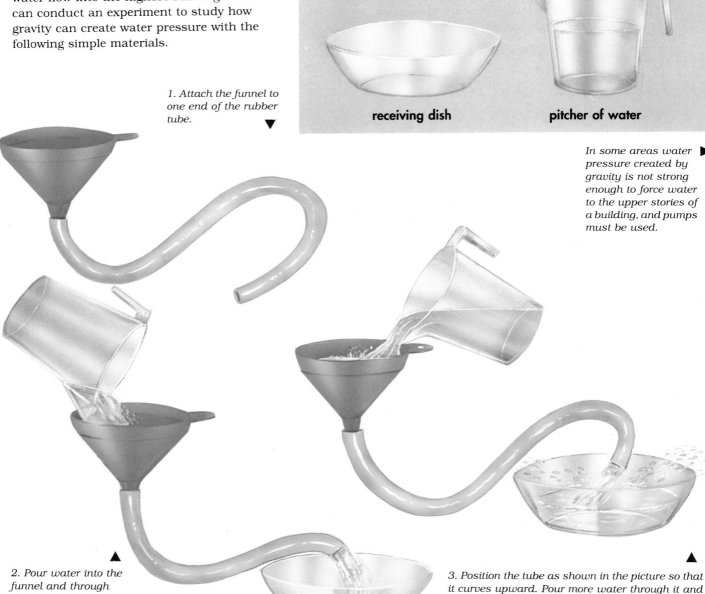

rubber hose

funnel

receiving dish

pitcher of water

1. Attach the funnel to one end of the rubber tube. ▼

In some areas water ▶ *pressure created by gravity is not strong enough to force water to the upper stories of a building, and pumps must be used.*

2. Pour water into the funnel and through the tube and watch how it enters the dish. ▲

3. Position the tube as shown in the picture so that it curves upward. Pour more water through it and observe how the water runs upward and out into the dish. ▲

Words to Remember

Adapted organism An organism that has successfully modified itself so as to be able to survive a change in its environment.

Additives Chemical substances that are added to food products to preserve them and to improve their color, odor, or texture.

Domesticate To tame wild animals so that they become used to living in or around the company of human beings.

Exploit To extract and make use of the Earth's natural resources.

Food chain A set of relationships established between living organisms in an ecosystem when they go in search of food.

Nomadic life A way of life characterized by continual roaming to assure survival, with no fixed home.

Renewable A natural resource that is never exhausted, that constantly renews itself.

Service gallery A subterranean gallery that collects, transports, and distributes a city's utility services, such as water, gas, or electricity.

Vacuum A space in which there is absolutely no material present.

Vibration A back-and-forth movement of air particles, water, or the ground in response to a stimulus.

Index